First World War
and Army of Occupation
War Diary
France, Belgium and Germany

59 DIVISION
Divisional Troops
Machine Gun Corps
25 Battalion
1 July 1918 - 30 September 1918

WO95/3017/10

The Naval & Military Press Ltd
www.nmarchive.com
Published in association with The National Archives

Published by

The Naval & Military Press Ltd

Unit 10 Ridgewood Industrial Park,

Uckfield, East Sussex,

TN22 5QE England

Tel: +44 (0) 1825 749494

www.naval-military-press.com

www.nmarchive.com

This diary has been reprinted in facsimile from the original. Any imperfections are inevitably reproduced and the quality may fall short of modern type and cartographic standards.

© Crown Copyright
Images reproduced by permission of The National Archives, London, England, 2015.

Contents

Document type	Place/Title	Date From	Date To
Heading	WO95/3017/10		
Heading	59 Div. Troops 25 BN Machine Gun Corps 1918 July Sept		
War Diary	Crequy	01/07/1918	17/07/1918
War Diary	Bois Des Dames	18/07/1918	23/07/1918
War Diary	Magnicourt	24/07/1918	24/07/1918
War Diary	Saulty	25/07/1918	26/07/1918
War Diary	In The Line Boyelles-Mercatel Section	27/07/1918	31/07/1918
War Diary	Mercatel Sector	01/08/1918	24/08/1918
War Diary	Liettres	25/08/1918	26/08/1918
War Diary	Lestrem Sector	27/08/1918	31/08/1918
Operation(al) Order(s)	Battalion Order No. 23	01/08/1918	01/08/1918
Operation(al) Order(s)	Battalion Order No. 24.	10/08/1918	10/08/1918
Operation(al) Order(s)	Battalion Order No. 25	15/08/1918	15/08/1918
Operation(al) Order(s)	Battalion Order No. 26	18/08/1918	18/08/1918
Operation(al) Order(s)	Battalion Order No. 27	21/08/1918	21/08/1918
Operation(al) Order(s)	Battalion Order No. 28	22/08/1918	22/08/1918
Operation(al) Order(s)	Battalion Order No. 29	23/08/1918	23/08/1918
Operation(al) Order(s)	Battalion Order No. 30	23/08/1918	23/08/1918
Operation(al) Order(s)	Battalion Order No. 32	23/08/1918	23/08/1918
Miscellaneous	No.25 Battn Machine Gun Cops		
Operation(al) Order(s)	Battalion Order No. 31	23/08/1918	23/08/1918
Operation(al) Order(s)	Battalion Order No. 33	25/08/1918	25/08/1918
War Diary	Lestrem Sector	01/09/1918	06/09/1918
War Diary	Laventie Sector	07/09/1918	30/09/1918
Operation(al) Order(s)	Battalion Order No. 35	01/09/1918	01/09/1918
Operation(al) Order(s)	Battalion Order No. 36		
Operation(al) Order(s)	Battalion Order No. 37		
Operation(al) Order(s)	Battalion Order No. 39	09/08/1918	09/08/1918
Operation(al) Order(s)	Battalion Order No. 40	09/09/1918	09/09/1918
Operation(al) Order(s)	Battalion Order No. 41	20/09/1918	20/09/1918
Operation(al) Order(s)	Battalion Order No. 42	25/09/1918	25/09/1918

spoon
3017
01/10 Q1

59 DIV TROOPS

25 BN MACHINE GUN CORPS

1918 JULY — SEPT

25th BATTALION. MACHINE GUN CORPS.

Army Form C. 2118.

WAR DIARY
INTELLIGENCE SUMMARY

Vol 6

Place	Date	Hour	Summary of Events and Information	Remarks and references to Appendices
CRÉQUY	1/7/18		Training P.T. Sykes etc & laying Section Drill	
"	2/7/18		Day devoted to Football match Officers v Sergeants followed by tug-of-war in the evening. Sports Entertainments. Draft of 13 Officers & 294 O.R. arrived (Lt. R.D. Ross, M.L. Anderson, J.S. Selbie, E. Salmon, W. Bartholomew, 2Lts. D. Walles, J. Gardiner, W.C. Webb, F. Shortleven, A.E. Welham, H.O.S. Whale, J.A. Young, A. Turnbull)	
"	3rd		Training. Decorations as follows awarded. Bar to M.C. Major D Campbell / M.C. 2Lt. T Bolam / " W.L. Johnstone / D.C.M. 131449 L.Cpl A. McSara.	
"	4th		Training. Gun cleaning. Belt filling etc.	
"	5th		Training. Lts. W Roscoe & W.M. Walles reported. Draft of 36 N.C.O.s & men arrived. Limber factory.	
"	6th		Training Capt C.F. Mackwell Leave to U.K. 9am – 1pm – Under Coy arrangements	

WAR DIARY
or
INTELLIGENCE SUMMARY.
(Erase heading not required.)

Army Form C. 2118.

Place	Date	Hour	Summary of Events and Information	Remarks and references to Appendices
CREQUY.	8/7/18		Training. 2nd Lt J Walker reported on arrival. Major H.T.P Williams M.C. leave to U.K.	
"	8th		Training. Capt. C.S. Mackrill appointed Adjutant vice Capt A.R. Maw M.C, to command D Coy, with effect 21-6-18.	
"	9th		Training. 9am – 1pm — Inter company arrangements. 1.A. Stephens etc.	
"	10th		Training. Route march combined with Visual training & Judging distances. 2nd Lt W Booth & A.H Frost reported to Battn.	
"	11th		Training. 2nd Lts A.E Yull & A Yull joined Battn.	
"	12th		Training. Lt F.R. Dyson M.C. leave to U.K. Major A.W.H Sim DSO, M.C. returned from sick leave. 9 – 1 — Elementary training. 1 Section by section officers.	
"	13th		Training, and Elementary training. 9am – 1pm —	

Army Form C. 2118.

WAR DIARY
or
INTELLIGENCE SUMMARY.
(Erase heading not required.)

Instructions regarding War Diaries and Intelligence Summaries are contained in F. S. Regs., Part II. and the Staff Manual respectively. Title pages will be prepared in manuscript.

Place	Date	Hour	Summary of Events and Information	Remarks and references to Appendices
CREQUI	14/7/18		Church Parade	
"	15th		Training. Elementary Gun drill etc.	
"	16th		Training. Transport moved by road to BOIS DES DAMES. Draft of 16 NCOs arrived from Base Depot. 2nd Lt Bolam on leave to UK	Appendix I
"	17th		Battalion moved by lorry to 1st Army reserve in BOIS DES DAMES. Took over bivouac camp in wood	Appendix I
BOIS DES DAMES	18th		Training. The following officers joined Battalion Lt A. M. Scout M.C. Lt J. L. Ferris. 2nd Lt W. H. Robertson.	
"	19th	9am-1pm	Elementary Training. P.T.	
"	20		Sunday Church Parade	
"	21	9am-1pm 4-7:45	P.T. Musketry 10. Battery Drill	
"	22	9am-1pm 4:7:45	Musketry Elementary Battery Drill Range 10 C Coy Day Range. Reconnaissance of area used 1st Corps by Battalion Snr	
"	23		Battalion transferred to 3rd Army's allotted to 59th Div.	

Army Form C. 2118.

WAR DIARY
or
INTELLIGENCE SUMMARY.
(Erase heading not required.)

Instructions regarding War Diaries and Intelligence Summaries are contained in F. S. Regs, Part II. and the Staff Manual respectively. Title pages will be prepared in manuscript.

Place	Date	Hour	Summary of Events and Information	Remarks and references to Appendices
BOIS DES DAMES	23/9/1		Battalion moved to MAIZIÈRES area, as per Operation Order No 21. Marches 36 kilometres in town rain. Billets in MAGNICOURT C Coy in	Appendix II
MAGNICOURT	24th		Battalion moved by road to SAULTY. Distance 17 Kilometres. Capt E.G. Marshall reported from leave.	Appendix III
SAULTY	25"		Platoon Commanders etc. for taking over line on night 26/27. Coy Commanders visited line to reconnoitre.	
"	26"		Battalion relieved Nos 1 & 2 Companies 3 Canadian Machine Gun Bn in BOYELLES-MERCATEL sector. One Section of A Company caught by shell on way up. 2 NCOs killed 4 NCOs & men wounded.	Appendix IV
In the line BOYELLES-MERCATEL Sector	27"		Relief completed by 2.45 a.m. Two companies in the line B on right A on left. C Company in reserve at RIVIERE D Company in Corps reserve at RIVIERE. Battalion H.Q. at Bn HQ BASSEUX. Transport lines & QM stores at BAILLEULVAL. Very quiet day in the line.	
			Same disposed as follow: B Coy 1 Sect under Cpl Peters near railway N.E of Boisleux au Mont. 1 Sect under Cpl Carr in front of embankment at BaBsSEe 1 Sect under 2d Dallas in MERCATEL SWITCH. A Coy 1 Sect under Smith Webb in M.34.d.7 M.35.c.1 Pickmen in man of Mose & Sect under Et Yeomans & Hat Majore, 1 Sect under St Wallis at M.32.c & M.31.3/6.	

WAR DIARY
or
INTELLIGENCE SUMMARY.

Army Form C. 2118.

Place	Date	Hour	Summary of Events and Information	Remarks and references to Appendices
In the Bryeulle-Marcoing Sector	28th		Quiet day in the line. Harassing fire carried out by forward guns during night 27/28 on various targets. Crossroads, tracks etc.	
"	29th		Another quiet day. Usual harassing fire carried out	
"	30th		Quiet day in the line. Harassing fire carried out by forward guns. Lt. F.K. Dyson MC returned from leave.	
"	31st		Usual night firing carried out	

W. Maclure
Lieut Col.
Comdg. No. 25 Bn MGC

WAR DIARY or INTELLIGENCE SUMMARY

Army Form C. 2118.

25th Bn. M.G. Corps

August 1918

Third Army

Place	Date	Hour	Summary of Events and Information	Remarks and references to Appendices
MERCATEL Sector	1/8/18.		A & B Companies in the line. With the exception of the usual harassing fire by artillery the day was quiet. During the night 2 guns of A & 4 guns of B carried out harassing fire on tracks etc. N.E. BOIRY BECQUERELLE. Our artillery was more active than usual during the night.	
"	2/8/18.		Enemy artillery was active at intervals during the day in the area between FICHEUX & the railway. About 3.15 p.m. 4 H.V. shells fell near RIVIERE CHATEAU. Our night firing guns were quiet during the night. At the request of infantry commanders 4 guns of the night company were laid on gaps in our wire. Casualties 1 O.R. wounded.	
"	3/8/18		Quiet day. About 9 p.m. 20 4.2" shells fell in BLAIRVILLE. C Company relieved A & D Company relieved B. A & B moved back to RIVIERE after relief. B Coy became coy reserve. Night firing was carried out on BOIRY BECQUERELLE & tracks in neighbourhood. 1 bayonet leave to U.K.	Appendix I

WAR DIARY or INTELLIGENCE SUMMARY.

(Erase heading not required.)

Army Form C. 2118.

Place	Date	Hour	Summary of Events and Information	Remarks and references to Appendices
MERCATEL Sector	4/8/18		Hostile artillery more active than usual during the day. About 4 am between 20 & 30 4.2's fell in neighbourhood of CHAT MAIGRE. About 1h 20 to 25 heavy shrapnel shells burst over road leading to CHAT MAIGRE from FICHEUX. During the night $\not\in$ our night firing guns fired on reported new work along BOYELLES - MERCATEL road N of COJEUL	
"	5/8/18		Very quiet day. During the morning the Commanding Officer went round the line with the O.R.E. to arrange work to be done on emplacements. Major Williams returned from leave.	
"	6/8/18		4th G.O.C. inspected A & B Companies at RIVIERE during the afternoon. During the night enemy artillery was active on BOISIEUX AU MONT. A few gas shells fell making it necessary for respirators to be worn. Night firing was carried out by our MGs on BOIRY BECQUERELLE & new work along BOYELLES - MERCATEL road.	

WAR DIARY or INTELLIGENCE SUMMARY

Army Form C. 2118.

(Erase heading not required.)

Instructions regarding War Diaries and Intelligence Summaries are contained in F. S. Regs., Part II. and the Staff Manual respectively. Title Pages will be prepared in manuscript.

Place	Date	Hour	Summary of Events and Information	Remarks and references to Appendices
MERCATEL Section	7/8/18		Quiet day. Enemy aeroplanes were slightly more active than usual. 2 low flying E.A. crossed our lines during the day but were driven back by AA & MG fire. Harassing fire was carried out by forward guns during the night.	
"	8/8/18		BLAIRVILLE & FICHEUX were shelled intermittently throughout the day. About 4 pm 30 4.2in shells fell in Railway cutting NW of BOISLEUX. Night firing was carried out in cross roads in neighbourhood of BOIRY BECQUERELLE	
"	9/8/18		Between 4 & 4.45 am enemy put down a barrage on MERCATEL. Enemy artillery was active all day. Night firing was carried out by our guns on usual targets.	
"	10/8/18		Our artillery were very active all day. About 1.30 pm a huge column of black smoke was seen in direction of VIS-EN-ARTOIS. This continued for at least 2 hours. FICHEUX – BOISLEUX road & level crossing were shelled intermittently during the day. Our M.G's did not fire during the night.	

2449 Wt. W14957/M90 750,000 1/16 J.B.C. & A. Forms/C.2118/12.

WAR DIARY or INTELLIGENCE SUMMARY

Army Form C. 2118.

Place	Date	Hour	Summary of Events and Information	Remarks and references to Appendices
MERCATEL Sector	11/8/18		Inter-company relief was carried out during the night 11/12. A relieved C & B relieved D. Between 11 pm & midnight E.A. were active. A few bombs were dropped between BAILIEULVAL and BERLES AU BOIS. Harassing fire was carried out on various tracks etc near BOIRY BECQUERELLE. Casualties 1 OR wounded.	Appendix II
"	12/8/18		Very quiet day. We carried out usual harassing fire during the night.	
"	13/8/18		Enemy artillery active during the day. About 10.30 am several gas shells fell in BOISIEUX AU MONT. Between 11.45 pm & midnight enemy roads about 500 yds NW of BOISIEUX were shelled with gas shells. Night firing was carried out on road junction & tracks N of BOIRY BECQUERELLE. Casualties 1 OR wounded.	
"	14/8/18		Quiet day. A few gas shells fell near the railway in the neighbourhood of CHAT MAIGRE about 8.30 pm. No night firing was carried out by our guns. A conference was held at BLAIRVILLE QUARRY in the morning at which the following were present. G.O.C. in Brigade Commander, C.R.A. C.R.E. & Machine Gun Battalion commander	

WAR DIARY
or
INTELLIGENCE SUMMARY.
(Erase heading not required.)

Army Form C. 2118.

Place	Date	Hour	Summary of Events and Information	Remarks and references to Appendices
MERCATEL Section	15/8/16		Alterations in our position took place during the night 15/16. Harassing fire was carried out on cross roads & tracks in the neighbourhood of BOIRY BECQUERELLE	Appendix III
"	16/8/16		Intermittent shelling by enemy artillery all day. Usual night firing was carried out by our M.G. During the night several bombs were dropped in & near BOISLEUX AU MONT by enemy aeroplane	
"	17/8/16		Quiet day. No night firing was carried out by night company left company, A, fired on cross roads N. of BOIRY-BECQUERELLE	
"	18/8/16		Some of A Company's guns S of MERCATEL were shelled during the day. On account of infantry patrols A Company were unable to do any night firing. B Company carried out usual programme	
"	19/8/16		Inter Company relief took place during night 19/20. B Company became 1st Reserve & was placed at disposal of No 2 S.B. Bde G.O.C. Guards Division	Appendix IV

Army Form C. 2118.

WAR DIARY
or
INTELLIGENCE SUMMARY.
(Erase heading not required.)

Instructions regarding War Diaries and Intelligence Summaries are contained in F. S. Regs., Part II. and the Staff Manual respectively. Title pages will be prepared in manuscript.

Place	Date	Hour	Summary of Events and Information	Remarks and references to Appendices
MERCATEL Sector	20/8/18		Our Artillery very active throughout the day. Owing to Infantry patrols very little rifle fire from our own.	
	21/8/18		Enemy division on our right attacked early in morning. HAMELINCOURT & MOYENNEVILLE. B Company moved from RIVIERE to a position between BLAIRVILLE & RANSART. During the night 21/22 "B" Company relieved the left company of Guards Machine Gun Regt. B Coy HQ now at a sunken road about 600 yds S.W. of crucifix — FICHEUX. During the night enemy were very active on track across Bomb was dropped in RIVIERE BASSEUX, BAILLEULVAL. One enemy bombing machine was shot down in flames near ARRAS — DOULLENS road N.W. of WAILLY.	Appendix V
	22/8/18		Fairly quiet during the day. Arrangements were made during the evening to gun covering fire for the 156 Infantry Brigade during the early stages of their attack in the morning of the 23rd. Infantry of 59th Division relieved during the night by 56th & 52nd Divisions. Casualties 1 O.R. killed 1 wounded	Appendix VI

WAR DIARY
or
INTELLIGENCE SUMMARY.
(Erase heading not required.)

Army Form C. 2118.

Place	Date	Hour	Summary of Events and Information	Remarks and references to Appendices
MERCATEL Sector	23/8/18		Covering fire given by C & D companies during early stages of attack which was entirely successful. Hill 90 & BORY REDOUBTS were captured. 27 flew P.W. men were taken in AVESNES.	Appendix VII
			During the night B Company withdrew from the line to RIVIÈRE	Appendix VIII
			C & D Companies were also relieved & returned to RIVIÈRE Casualties 1 O.R. killed in action, 3 wounded	
" "	24/8/18		Battalion less transport entrained at SAULTY for LILLERS. Transport moved by road to ANVIN	Appendix IX / Appendix X
LIETTRES	25/8/18		Battalion detrained at LILLERS about 3 a.m. & marched to LIETTRES. Transport continued its march from ANVIN and arrived at LIETTRES late in the afternoon.	
"	26/8/18		Battalion relieved the 74th Bn M.G.C. in the LESTREM Sector. Coys 2nd in Commands A & D & Sig. & Intelligence officers went along to H.Q. 74 Battn by lorry at 10.30 am to reconnoitre B.O.R. & to all officers of Battalion at 9.45 am. Personnel of H.Q, C & D moved to LABIETTE Farm by bus. Owing to shortage of buses A & B Companies were unable to move.	Appendix XI / Appendix XII

Army Form C. 2118.

WAR DIARY
or
INTELLIGENCE SUMMARY.
(Erase heading not required.)

Instructions regarding War Diaries and Intelligence Summaries are contained in F. S. Regs., Part II. and the Staff Manual respectively. Title pages will be prepared in manuscript.

Place	Date	Hour	Summary of Events and Information	Remarks and references to Appendices
LESTREM Sect.	27/8/16		A & B companies moved by lorry from LILLERS & arrived about 11am. Quiet day in the line. There was a little artillery fire from the enemy in the afternoon. Several fires were observed behind the enemy lines during the night.	
"	28/8/16		Fairly quiet day. Enemy shelled MERVILLE during the morning. No enfilade firing was carried out during the night.	
"	29/8/16		Numerous fires were observed behind the enemy's lines throughout the day. PARADIS road was lightly shelled throughout the morning. In the evening ABBEY road was shelled.	
"	30/8/16		Owing to enemy's withdrawal, D Company guns were moved forward during the day to positions along the line ABBEY ROAD – L'EPINETTE. Company Headquarters moved to LA CALONNE.	

Army Form C. 2118.

WAR DIARY
or
INTELLIGENCE SUMMARY.
(Erase heading not required.)

Instructions regarding War Diaries and Intelligence Summaries are contained in F. S. Regs., Part II. and the Staff Manual respectively. Title pages will be prepared in manuscript.

Place	Date	Hour	Summary of Events and Information	Remarks and references to Appendices
LESTREM Sector	31/8/18.		During the morning the enemy tried Rigged tried to cross the River LAWE but were held up in the morning. During the afternoon however they succeeded in pushing forward. D Company H.Q. moved to a position 500 yards S of LESTREM church on the LOBON road. D Company moved in the evening with 176 Brigade in support to line MEURILLON, EPINETTE, LA CIX MARMEUSE. 7 overture transmons Headquarters was situated at junction of PARADISE ROAD & LESTREM STREET.	

W. Parker
Lieut Col commanding
25th Battalion Machine Gun Corps.

SECRET   War Diary   Appendix I   COPY No. 11

25th BATTALION M.G. CORPS
BATTALION ORDER No. 23

Reference Maps - Sheets 51c. S.E. & 51 b. S.W. 1:20,000   1.8.1918

1. Inter company reliefs will be carried out in accordance with the following table on the night 3rd/4th August 1918.

        C Company will relieve A Company
        D   do.   "   "   B   "

   On completion of relief A & B Companies will move back into reserve at RIVIERE & will occupy the billets vacated by "C" & "D" Coys, respectively.

   B Company will be in Corps Reserve and will hold itself in readiness to move at short notice.

2. All maps, trench stores, S.A.A., tools, etc, will be handed over.

3. All details of relief will be arranged between O's C. Coys. concerned, & a copy of Coy relief orders will be sent to Battalion Orderly Room.

4. Sections of A & B Coys. will utilise limbers of relieving Sections of C & D Coys. to carry gun equipment not handed over, to transport lines at RIVIERE. After which these limbers will proceed to the lines at BAILLEULVAL. O's C. A & B Coys will arrange to move their transport from BAILLEULVAL to transport lines RIVIERE 2 hours before completion of relief.

5. O's C. C & D Coys will each leave one officer in billets at RIVIERE to hand over to O's C. A & B Coys. the reserve gun positions.

6. Completion of relief will be wired to Battalion H.Q. using code word "AGAIN"

7. Acknowledge.

Copy No.			
1.	C.O.	9.	R.S.M.
2.	O.C. A Coy.	10.	File
3.	" B "	11.	War }
4.	" C "	12.	Diary }
5.	" D "	13.	59th Div. G.
6.	" H.Q. "	14.	177 Infantry Bde.
7.	T.O.	15.	178 "
8.	Q.M.		

C.G. Machell
CAPT. & ADJT.
25 BATTALION. M.G. CORPS

Appendix 4

SECRET.   Copy No. 14

BATTALION ORDER NO. 24.

~~S..... ....~~

Reference Maps.- Shts. 51.c.S.E, 1/20,000
              "   51.b.S.W.   "   10. 8. 18.

1. Inter-Company Reliefs will be carried out in accordance with the following table on the night ~~xxx/xxxxxx~~ 11th/12th August, 1918.

    "A" Company will relieve "C" Company.
    "B"   "   "   "   "D"   "

    On completion of Relief "C" and "D" Companies will move back into Reserve at RIVIERE and will occupy the Billets vacated by "A" and "B" Companies respectively.

    "D" Company will be in Corps Reserve and will hold itself in readiness to move at short notice.

2. All Maps, Trench Stores, S.A.A., Tools, etc, will be handed over.

3. All details of Relief will be arranged between O's C. Companies concerned, and a copy of Company Relief orders will be sent to Battalion Orderly Room.

4. Sections of C. and D. Companies will utilise Limbers of relieving Sections of A and B. Companies, to carry Gun Equipment not handed over, to Transport Lines at RIVIERE, afetr which these Limbers will proceed to the Lines at BAILLEULVAL. O's C. "C" and "D" Companies will arrange to move their Transport from BAILLEULVAL to Transport Lines at RIVIERE 2 hours before completion of relief.

5. O's C. "A" and "B" Companies will each leave one Officer to hand over Billets in RIVIERE.

6. Completion of "Relief" will be wired to Battalion H.Q. using Code Word "EASY"

7. A C K N O W L E D G E.

                                            Mackule
                                            Capt. & Adjutant,
                                            No. 2B. Battalion, M.Gun Corps.

Issued at -
    "   by - Battn. Runner.
    "   to-
    Copy. No. 1. C.O.
     "   "   2. O.C. A. Company.   9. R.S.M.
     "   "   3.   "   B.   "   10. File.
     "   "   4.   "   C.   "   11. 59th Div.
     "   "   5.   "   D.   "   12. 176th Infty. Bde.
     "   "   6. Sig. Officer.   13. 178th   do
     "   "   7. Transport Officer   14/15. War Diary.
     "   "   8. Quartermaster.   16. 56= Bn. MGC.
                                           17. 4= Guards MG Regt.

Appendix II

SECRET.　　　　　　　　　　　　　　　　　　　　　Copy No. 14

BATTALION ORDER NO. 24.

Reference Maps.- Shts. 51.c.S.E, 1/20,000
　　　　　　　　"　51.b.S.W.　　"　　　　　　　　　10. 8. 18.

1.　　Inter-Company Reliefs will be carried out in accordance with the following table on the night ~~2nd/3rd~~ 11th/12th August. 1918.

　　　　"A" Company will relieve "C" Company.
　　　　"B"　　"　　　"　　　"D"　　"

　　On completion of Relief "C" and "D" Companies will move back into Reserve at RIVIERE and will occupy the Billets vacated by "A" and "B" Companies respectively.

　　"D" Company will be in Corps Reserve and will hold itself in readiness to move at short notice.

2.　　All Maps, Trench Stores, S.A.A., Tools, etc, will be handed over.

3.　　All details of Relief will be arranged between O's C. Companies concerned, and a copy of Company Relief orders will be sent to Battalion Orderly Room.

4.　　Sections of C. and D. Companies will utilise Limbers of relieving Sections of A and B. Companies, to carry Gun Equipment not handed over, to Transport Lines at RIVIERE, afetr which these Limbers will proceed to the Lines at BAILLEULVAL. O's C. "C" and "D" Companies will arrange to move their Transport from BAILLEULVAL to Transport Lines at RIVIERE 2 hours before completion of relief.

5.　　O's C. "A" and "B" Companies will each leave one Officer to hand over Billets in RIVIERE.

6.　　Completion of "Relief" will be wired to Battalion H.Q. using Code Word "EASY"

7.　　A C K N O W L E D G E.

　　　　　　　　　　　　　　　　　　　　　　　Mackenzie
　　　　　　　　　　　　　　　　　　　　　　　Capt. & Adjutant

Issued at :-

add to Para 2 :

All details of work on hand or proposed to be handed over.

In Para I read :
A Company will relieve C Company in the left subsector.
B Company will relieve D Company in the right subsector.

17　　4 Guards MG Regt.

Appendix III

SECRET.   Copy No. 14

No. 25. Battalion, Machine Gun Corps.

BATTALION ORDER NO. 25.
@ ⓒⓒⓒⓒⓒⓒⓒⓒⓒⓒⓒⓒⓒⓒⓒⓒⓒⓒⓒⓒ

1. The following alterations in Machine Gun positions will take place on the night of 15/16th August 1918.

2. **LEFT GROUP.**

   (a) 2 Guns at present in Tunnel at M.33.a.75.20. will be relieved by 2 Guns at present at M.34.a.10.80. and will move to Tunnel at M.21.c.65.10.
   Temporary emplacements will be made on bank in hedge on Eastern side of Railway embankment. These Guns will be numbered S.39. and S.40.
   Fighting Map for new position will be sent to O.C. Left Group by 12 noon, 15th August. Section Officers will see that teams are acquainted with the Field of Fire, etc, before dark on the 15th August.
   2 Guns in Tunnel at M.27.c.70.68. will remain in present position and will be numbered S.41. and S.42.
   Section Headquarters for this Section will remain in present position.

   (b) 2 Guns at present at M.34.a.10.80. will take over the position in the Tunnel at M.33.a.75.20. These Guns will be called S.43. and S.44.
   Range Cards, Battle Lines, etc, will be handed over by Section Officers concerned before dark on 15th August.
   2 Guns at present at M.28.c.30.15. will move to CHAMPAGNE emplacement at M.33.b.68.70. These Guns will be numbered S.25. and S.26. Pending completion of Saps to Gun positions these Guns will be kept in the Dugout, but will fight from the positions already marked out.
   Fighting Map for new position will be sent to O.C. Left Group by 12 noon 15th August. Section Officer will see that teams are acquainted with the Field of Fire, etc, before dark on 15th August.
   Section H.Q. for this Section will be in Tunnel at M.33.a.75.20.

3. **RIGHT GROUP.**

   (a) F.53. and F.54. will move from present positions at S.5.c.10.82. to Champagne emplacement at S.5.c.38.78. Pending completion of Saps to to Gun positions these Guns will be kept in Dug-out but will fight from the positions already marked out.

   (b) F.55. and F.56. will move from present positions at S.4.b.80.62. temporally to Champagne emplacement at S.4.b.0.2. Pending completion of this emplacement these Guns will fight from the positions already marked out.
   Fighting Maps for all new positions will be sent to O.C.Right Group by 12 noon 15th August. O.C.Section concerned will see that the teams are acquainted with the fields of Fire before dark on 15th August.
   Section H.Q. for this Section will remain in present location.

(2)

BATTALION ORDER NO.25. (continued).

4. Officers Commanding Groups will see that the 16 Filled Belt Boxes, 5 Boxes S.A.A. and other stores laid down in Battn! Standing Orders, Para. 24. are at the new positions before Dawn on August 16th.

5. A C K N O W L E D G E.   (Companies only)

15.8.18.

Sherehuele
Caporadi
for
Lieut.Col.,
Commanding, No.25.Battalion, M.G.Corps.

Issued by - Battalion Runner.
Distribution :-

    Copy. No. 1.   C.O.
            2.   2nd in Command.
            3.   O.C; A.Company.
            4.   O.C; B;   "
            5.   O.C. C.   "
            6.   O.C; D.   "
            7.   G.S. 176th Infty Bde.
            8.   "   178th   "   "
            9.   Guards M.G.Battalion.
          10.   56th Battn, M.Gun Corps.
          11.   M.G.O. VI Corps.
          12.   Intelligence Officer.
          13.   File.
          14/15. War Diary.

SECRET. Appendix IV   COPY NO. 16

BATALION ORDER NO.

Ref. Map. — Shts. 51c.S.E. 1/20,000.
         "   51b.S.W. 1/20,000.   18.8.18.

1.   Inter-Company Reliefs will be carried out in accordance with the following table on the night 19th/20th August 1918.

   "C" Company will relieve "A" Company in LEFT SUB-SECTOR.

   "D" Company will relieve "B" Company in RIGHT SUB-SECTOR.

   On completion of Relief "A" and "B" Companies will move back into Reserve at RIVIERE and will occupy the Billets vacated by "C" and "D" Companies respectively.

   "B" Company will be in Corps Reserve and will hold itself in readiness to move at short notice.

2.   All details of work in hand or proposed, all Maps, Trench Stores, S.A.A. Tools, etc, will be handed over.

3.   All details of Relief will be arranged between O.C' Companies concerned, and a copy of Company Relief Orders will be sent to Battalion Orderly Room.

4.   Sections of A. & B. Companies will utilise Limbers of relieving Sections of C. & D. Companies, to carry Gun Equipment not handed over to Transport Lines at RIVIERE, after which these Limbers will proceed to the Lines at BAILLEULVAL. O's C. "A" and "B" Companies will arrange to move their Transport from BAILLEULVAL to Transport Lines at RIVIERE 2 hours before completion of relief.

5.   O's C. "C" and "D" Companies will each leave one Officer to hand over Billets in RIVIERE.

6.   Completion of Relief" will be wired to Battalion H.Q. using Code words "NO WIND".

7.   A C K N O W L E D G E. (Companies only)

                                                    [signature]
                                                    Capt. & Adjutant,
Issued at   by D.R.   No.25.Battn. Machine Gun Corps.

Distribution :-

   Copy No. 1.   O.C.   Copy. No. 10. 59th Division.
    "   " 2.   O.C. A. Company.   "   " 11. 176th Infty Bde.
    "   " 3.   "   B.   "   "   " 12. 177th   "   "
    "   " 4.   "   C.   "   "   " 13. 15th Bn. M.G.C.
    "   " 5.   "   D.   "   "   " 14. 4th Bn. Guards M.G.
    "   " 6.   Sig. Officer.   "   " 15. File.
    "   " 7.   Transport Officer.   "   " 16/17. War Diary.
    "   " 8.   Quartermaster.   "   " 18. 2nd in Command.
    "   " 9.   R.S.M.

Appendix V

SECRET   Copy No. 16

NO. 25. BATTALION, MACHINE GUN CORPS.

BATTALION ORDER NO. 27.

21st August 1918.

Ref. Map.- Shts 51c S.E. 1/20,000.
         "   51b.S.W. 1/20,000.

1. "B" Company will relieve the left Company of the 4th Battalion, Guards Machine Gun Regt, on night 21st/22nd August 1918.

2. Relief to be carried out in accordance with orders issued by 4th Bn, Guards Machine Gun Regt.

3. Trench Stores, Maps, etc, to be taken over.

4. The Defence Scheme of 4th Bn, Guards M.G.Regt, will be acted on pending issue of fresh instructions.

5. On completion of Relief O.C."B" Company will send direct to Battn' Headquarters a Map shewing dispositions, HQ's of Sections and Company, etc,, He will arrange to keep one Runner at Headquarters, "D" Company. (25th Bn. M.G.C.).

6. A C K N O W L E D G E. (Companies only.)

                                                 Capt. & Adjt,
                                       No.25.Battn, Machine Gun Corps.

Issued at   by D.R.
Distribution :-

     Copy. No. 1.   O.C.
         "   2.   O.C.A.Company.
         "   3.   " B "
         "   4.   " C "
         "   5.   " D "
         "   6.   Signalling Officer.
         "   7.   Transport Officer.
         "   8.   Quartermaster.
         "   9.   59th Division.
         "   10.   177th Infty Bde.
         "   11.   178th " "
         "   12.   4th Bn. Guards M.G.Regt.
         "   13.   2nd in Command.
         "   14.   R.S.M.
         "   15.   File.
         "   16/17. War Diary.

S E C R E T.

COPY NO. 13

25th BATTALION, MACHINE GUN CORPS.

OPERATION ORDER NO.28.

Ref.Map. Shts. 51c.S.E. 1.20.000.
         " 51b.S.W. "

August 22nd 1918.

1. The 25th Battalion, Machine Gun Corps will co-operate in the attack of the 156th Infantry Brigade tomorrow 23rd August 1918 by Indirect Covering Fire during the earlier stages of the advance.

2. The following alterations will be made in the dispositions of the Machine Guns now in the Line.
    RIGHT GROUP. - The Section at present occupying R.53., R.54., R.57. and R.58. in S.1.b. will move to positions in the Sunken Road from S.5.c.3.7. to S.5.c.3.0.
    Two Guns at present in S.4.b.0.2. will also move up to positions alongside the other 2 Guns of the Section in S.5.c.3.6.
    These 8 Guns will be under the Command of Capt.WALLIS, whose Headquarters will be at S.5.c.3.6. These 8 Guns will be used to give Covering Fire onto certain localities.
    Details of Targets and times of fire will be communicated later to O.C.RIGHT GROUP.

3. LEFT GROUP. - The Section at present occupying R.55., R.56., R.59., and R.60., will move up to positions in TEAK LANE extension about M.35.c.5.8.
    The 2 Guns at F.59. & F.60. will move up to positions near F.57. and F.58. about M.35.c.6.8.
    These 8 Guns will fire under the Command of Lieut.BARTHOLOMEW, "C"Company, whose Headquarters will be at M.35.c.65.70.
    These 8 Guns will be used to give Covering Fire onto certain localities.
    Details of Targets and times of Fire will be communicated later to O.C.LEFT GROUP., In addition these Guns will be responsible for covering the Left Flank of the attack by Direct Fire, if required, during consolidation.

4. After the attack, the 16 Guns mentioned in paras. 2. & 3., will will remain in position and will be Rear Guns.

5. O's C. Left and Right Group will arrange to get extra Belts, Barrels and Water up to these Guns to-night.
    It is estimated that the period and rate of Fire will be:-

    For 12 minutes at the rate of 1 Belt per 3 minutes.
    For 20 minutes at the rate of 1 Belt per 10 minutes.

Subsequently every opportunity will be taken of engaging Targets with Direct Fire.

6. The Section Headquarter in Sunken Road at M.35.a.20.10. will be the forward Dump for "B" Company, 52nd Machine Gun Battalion, who will go forward to consolidate. In addition forward Dumps of filled Belts, Water, S.A.A., Spare Parts, etc, will be formed as under for the use of "B" Company, 52nd Machine Gun Battalion:-

    By O.C. Left Group at Trench Junction in M.35.d.90.50.
    By O.C. Right Group - in Sunken Road at S.5.c.3.6.

OPERATION ORDER NO.28. continued)

6. (Contd)   Men of "B" Company 52nd Battalion, M.G.C. will use Rifle Butts, near this point as a Guide, when returning to this Dump.   O.C.Right Group will arrange to guide them from Rifle Butts to the Dump.

7.   O.C.Left Group will arrange to guide the Limbers of "B" Company, 52nd Machine Gun Battalion from BRETENCOURT to debussing point at M.33.c.0.0.
On arrival of the personnel in Busses at that point, one Officer from Left Group will guide Limbers and personnel to old Section Headquarter in Sunken Road at M.35.a.20.10.
Time of arrival of Busses to be notified later.

8.   The Section of "A" Company now in positions R.61., R.62., R.63., and R.64., will rejoin "A" Company in RIVIERE tonight.   Pack Transport will be used for moving Guns, Belts, etc.

9.   Watches will be synchronised at H.Q. 156th Brigade which will be in BLAIREVILLE QUARRY.   Hour of Zero must be obtained from H.Q. 156th Brigade.

10.   A C K N O W L E D G E.   (Companies only)

[signature]

Capt. & Adjutant,
No.25.Battalion, Machine Gun Corps.

Issued at *[handwritten]* by S.D.R.
Distribution:-
    Copy No.1;   C.O.
    "   " 2.   2nd in Command.
    "   " 3.   O.C.A.Company.
    "   " 4.   O.C.C.   "
    "   " 5.   " D.   "
    "   " 6.   G.S. 59th Division.
    "   " 7.   177th Infantry Brigade.
    " v " 8.   176th   "   "
    "   " 9.   H.Q. 52nd Battn, M.G.C.
    "   " 10.   "B" Coy.   do
    "   " 11.   156th Infty. Brigade.
    "   " 12.   File.
    "   " 13/14. War Diary.
    "   " 15.   Signalling Officer.

Appendix VII

SECRET.
COPY NO. 17

25th BATTALION, MACHINE GUN CORPS.

BATTALION ORDER NO.29.

Ref. Sheets. 51c.S.E. 1:20,000.
" 51b.S.W. 1:20,000.

August 23nd 1918.

1. "B" Company, 25th Battn' Machine Gun Corps. will withdraw tonight, 23rd inst, from 56th Divisional Area. (Authy:- 56th Div.)

2. This Company will get in touch with Lieut.Col. JERVIS. D.S.O., O.C. 56th Battn' M.G.Corps, who will be at 56th Division, Advanced Headquarters in Quarry at X.3.d.5.7. and arrange about the handing over of Stores, etc in the Line.

3. "B" Company, after withdrawal will return to RIVIERE. O.C. "A"Company, 25th Battn, M.G.Corps will arrange accommodation for "B" Company in RIVIERE. Rations for "B" Company will be left in charge of "A" Company.

4. "C" and "D" Companies, 25th Bn, M.G.Corps, will remain in the Line until night of 24th/25th when they will be relieved by a Company from the 52nd Battn. M.G.Corps. Details of Relief to be arranged between O.C.Companies concerned.

5. All Maps, Trench Stores, will be handed over and receipts forwarded to this Office.

6. Relief complete will be wired to Battn. H.Q. using the following phrase :- " Your B.R.120. received at ....".

7. Orders as to disposal of C. & D.Companies 25th Bn, M.G.C. on relief, will be issued later.

8. A.Company, and Battn.H.Q. will remain in present locations. i.e. RIVIERE and BASSEUX respectively.

9. A C K N O W L E D G E. (Companies only.)

Capt. & Adjt,
No.25.Battn, Machine Gun Corps.

Issued at......... by D.R.
Distribution:-

Copy. No. 1. C.O.
" " 2. 2nd in Command.
" " 3. O.C.A.Company.
" " 4. " B. "
" " 5. " C. "
" " 6. " D. "
" " 7. Signalling Officer.
" " 8. Quartermaster.
" " 9. Transport Officer.
" " 10. 56th Division.
" " 11. 52nd "
" " 12. 56th M.G.Battalion.
" " 13. 52nd " "
" " 14. 156th Infty. Brigade.
" " 15. R.S.M.
" " 16. File.
" " 17/18. War Diary.

Appendix VIII

SECRET   NO. 25. BATTALION, MACHINE GUN CORPS.   COPY NO. 18

BATTALION ORDER NO. 30.

23rd August 1918.

Ref. Sheet. 51.c.S.E. 1.20.000
"   51.b.S.W. 1.20.000.

1. "C" & "D" Companies, 25th Battn' Machine Gun Corps, will be relieved on night 23rd/24th by Companies of 52nd Battn' M.G.C.

2. Details of this Relief will be arranged by the O.C. Companies concerned.

3. On relief "C" & "D" Companies will proceed to RIVIERE, at which place Billets will be arranged for by O.C. "A" Company. O.C. "A" Company will also arrange to have Guides on the Cross Roads at R.27.c.25.20, to guide "C" & "D" Companies to Billets.

4. All Maps, Trench Stores, etc, to be handed over.

5. Relief Complete will be wired to Battalion H.Q.s using the following phrase:- "YOUR B.R.125. received at ...."

6. On August 24th the Battalion will move by Train, Transport by Road, to the WAIL Area. Orders as to Entrainment and move of Transport will be issued separately.

7. Battalion Order No.29. is cancelled with the exception of paras 1, 2, & 3. which concern "B" Company, 25th Battn. M.G.C.

8. A C K N O W L E D G E. (Companies only).

                                                 C.G. Mackrell
                                                Capt. & Adjutant,

Issued at 6.30pm by S.D.R.   No.25.Battalion, Machine Gun Corps.
Distribution:-

Copy No.	
1.	C.O.
2.	2nd in Command.
3.	O.C. A. Company.
4.	" B. "
5.	" C. "
6.	" D. "
7.	Signalling Officer.
8.	Quartermaster.
9.	Transport Officer.
10.	52nd Division.
11.	52nd Bn. M.G.C.
12.	156th Infty Bde.
13.	56th Division.
14.	56th Bn. M.G.C.
15.	File.
16.	M.O.
17.	R.S.M.
18/19.	War Diary.

COPY No. ....

To. 25. BATTALION, MACHINE GUN CORPS.

BATTALION ORDER NO. 30.
─────────────

Ref.Sheet. Sh.3.G.L. 1.20.000.   23rd August, 1917.
         "   51.B.& W. 1.20.000.

1. "C" & "D" Companies, 25th Batth, Machine Gun Corps, will be
    relieved on night 23rd/24th by Companies of 22nd Batth, M.G.C.

2. Details of this Relief will be arranged by the O.C. Companies
    concerned.

3. On relief "C" & "D" Companies will proceed to RIVIERE, at
    which place Billets will be arranged for by O.C. "A" Company.
    O.C. "A" Company will also arrange to have Guides on the
    Cross Roads at N.27.c.25.20. to guide "C" & "D" Companies to
    Billets.

4. All Maps, Trench Stores, etc. to be handed over.

5. Relief Complete will be wired to Battalion H.Q.s using the
    following phrase:- "YOUR B.R.125. received at ...."

6. On August 24th the Battalion will move by Train, Transport by
    Road, to the WAIL Area. Orders, as to Entrainment and move of
    Transport will be issued separately.

7. Battalion Order No.29. is cancelled with the exception of paras.
    1, 2, & 3. which concern "B" Company, 25th Batth, M.G.C.

8. A C K N O W L E D G E. (Companies only).

                                                    Marshall
                                                 Capt. & Adjutant,
Issued at ....by S.D.R.   No.25.Battalion, Machine Gun Corps.
Distribution:-

    Copy No.1. O.C.
      "   2.   2nd in Command.
      "   3.   O.C. A.Company.
      "   4.   " B.   "
      "   5.   " C.   "
      "   6.   " D.   "
      "   7.   Signalling Officer.
      "   8.   Quartermaster.
      "   9.   Transport Officer.
      "   10.   22nd Division.
      "   11.   22nd Bn. M.G.C.
      "   12.   166th Infy Bde.
      "   13.   56th Division.
      "   14.   56th Bn. M.G.C.
      "   15.   File.
      "   16.   M.O.
      "   17.   R.S.M.
      "   18/19. War Diary.

SECRET.   Appendix IX   Copy No. 13

NO. 25. BATTALION MACHINE GUN CORPS.

BATTALION ORDER NO.32.

Ref.Sheet.51.c.S.E. 1.20.000.   23rd August.1918.

1. The Battalion, less Transport, will move to SAULTY Station tomorrow August 24th for Entrainment to WAIL Area, according to the attached table.

2. Battalion H.Q's, A, B, C, & D, Companies will entrain by No.6.Train which leaves SAULTY at 6.45.p.m.

3. The journey is expected to take 3½ to 4 hours.

4. Entraining will be in charge of Lieut. DYSON. M.C. who will report to R.T.O. at SAULTY 1½ hours before Train is due start. He will take a complete Marching Out state showing numbers of Officers, Men, etc., so that accommodation can be checked by R.T.O.

5. 2nd Lieut.T.BOLAM. M.C., Interpreter, and 6 men from Battn' H.Q's to represent Companies, etc., will proceed by Train leaving SAULTY at 11.40.a.m. 24th inst. Bicycles and 1 days ration will be taken. On arrival he will report to D.A.A.G., 59th Division who will allot Billeting Area.
This Party will report to Battalion Orderly Room BASSEUX at 9.a.m.
The Billeting Party will meet the Battalion at Detraining Station.

6. The following is laid down for Train Journey:-

   (a) No man will be allowed to leave the Train without permission.

   (b) Doors of Carriages on Right hand side of Train. When on main Line will be kept closed.

   (c) Picquets will be detailed to enforce Para 1. "A" Company will detail picquet for front of Train and "D" Company the picquet for rear of Train. Each Post consists of 1 N.C.O. & 3 men.

   (d) No Fires or Braziers will be allowed in Trucks.

7. Companies will collect all Dixies from Cookers, etc which will be necessary for making Tea on arrival at SAULTY and dump them at A.Coy. H.Q's.
A Motor Lorry will be at RIVIERE at 12 noon, for the purpose of conveying these to SAULTY Station. Cooks will proceed with the Lorry and prepare Tea for Battalion on arrival. A Loading Party will be provided for loading dixies.

8. ACKNOWLEDGE.

                             Capt. & Adjt,
                             No.25.Battn, Machine Gun Corps.

Issued at 11.45 p.m. by S.D.R.
Distribution:-
Copy. No.1. C.O.
      2. 2nd in Command.
      3. O.C. A.Company.
      4. " B. "
      5. " C. "
      6. " D. "
      7. Signalling Officer.
      8. Transport Officer.
      No.9. Quartermaster
      10. Medical Officer
      11. R.S.M.
      12. File.
      13/14. War Diary.

No. 25. BATTN'. MACHINE GUN CORPS.

MARCH TABLE to accompany B.O. No.32.

Company and Order of March.	Starting Point.	Companies pass Starting Point at:-	Route.
Battalion. Headquarters.	W.3.b.35.70.	2.25.p.m.	BAILLEULVAL.
A. Company.	do	2.30.p.m.	BAC DU SUD.
B. "	do	2.36.p.m.	SAULTY.
C. "	do	2.42.p.m.	
D. "	do	2.48.p.m.	

SECRET.   COPY NO. 13

NO. 25. BATTALION, MACHINE GUN CORPS.
BATTALION ORDERS NO.31.

23rd August 1918.

Ref. Sht.51.c.S.E. 1.20.000

1. The Transport of the Battalion will move on August 24th in accordance with the following Table:-

From.	To.	Starting Point.	Time. pass S.P.	Route.
RIVIERE & BASSEUX.	To be notified later.	W.3.b.35.70.	12.30.p.m.	AVESNES.le COMTE. REBREUVIETTE FREVENT.

2. A Halt will be made for 2 hours in the neighbourhood of REBREUVIETTE, care being taken to move off the main road on to fields that have been harvested.

3. Lieut.W.G.HINDS will command the Battalion Group.

4. Regulation distances to be maintained on the line of march.

5. A C K N O W L E D G E.

                                                 Capt. & Adjt.,
                                                 No.25.Battn, M.Gun Corps.

Issued at: 4.5a. by D.R.
Distribution.:-

        Copy.No.1.   C.O.
              2.   2nd in Command.
              3.   O.C. A.Company.
              4.   "   B.   "
              5.   "   C.   "
              6.   "   D.   "
              7.   Signalling Officer.
              8.   Quartermaster.
              9.   Transport Officer.
             10.   Medical Officer.
             11.   R.S.M.
             12.   File.
             13/14. War Diary.

Appendix XI

SECRET.   25TH BATTALION, MACHINE GUN CORPS.   Copy No. 16

BATTALION ORDER NO.33.

25th August 18

Ref.Sheet.36a.N.E. } 1.20.000.
"   36a.S.E. }

1. The Battalion will relieve the 74th Battn, Machine Gun Corps in the Line on the night of 26th/27th August 1918.

2. Dispositions will be as follows:-

   OUTPOST LINE (Approx: K.36.Central to R.20.00) D.Company.

   LINE OF RETENTION. (Approx: Q.1. to Q.20.). - C.Company.

   IN RESERVE - "A" and "B" Companies.

3. Personnel of Battalion Headquarters, "C" and "D" Companies will move tomorrow by Bus to LAVIETTE Farm. Details will be notified later.
   The Transport of above will move by road and join personnel at LAVIETTE Farm. Hour of Starting to be notified later.

4. Details of Relief of Companies in the Line will be arranged by the O's C.Companies concerned.

5. A Bus will leave Battalion Headquarters,LIETTRES at 9.a.m. tomorrow August 26th to convey O's C. "C" & "D" Companies a   any Section Officers of these Companies whom it is desired to send, 2nd in Command "A" & "B" Companies, Signalling Officer, and Intelligence Officer, to the Headquarters of 74th Battalion, Machine Gun Corps at LAVIETTE FARM.

6. Orders as to move of "A" & "B" Companies will be issued later

7. Battalion Headquarters, and the two Reserve Companies will be at LAVIETTE, about P.27.Central.

8. Relief of Infantry in the Line will take place in Line on Night 27th/28th August. Dispositions will be :-

   OUTPOST LINE - 177th Infantry Brigade.
   LINE OF RETENTION. - 178th Infantry Brigade.
   RESERVE. -   176th Infantry Brigade.
   Headquarters of Infty Brigade in Outpost Line will be at Q.19.a.7.6.

9. All Maps, Trench Stores, etc, will be taken over and complete Lists of these will be rendered to Orderly Room by 10.a.m. 29th inst.

10. Relief Complete will be reported to Battalion Headquarters by method of Communication to be arranged tomorrow at LAVIETTE Farm, using the Phrase :- "Your B.S. 1900 received at........"

11. A C K N O W L E D G E. (Companies only).

Capt. & Adjt,
No.25.Bn, Machine Gun Corps.

Issued at...... by D.R.
Distribution:-
   Copy No.1.. C.O.   Copy.No.8. Transport Offr
   "   2.   2nd in Command.   "   9.   Q.M.
   "   3   O.C. A.Company.   "   10.   C.M.G.O.
   "   4   "   B.   "   "   11.   59th Div.
   "   5   "   C.   "   "   12.   177th Bde.
   "   6   "   D.   "   "   13.   175th Bde. 178
   "   7   Signalling Officer.   " 14/ 74th M.G.Battn.
   "   18.   R.S.M.   15.   File.
                                       " 16/17. War Diary.

25th Bn M.G.C.

WAR DIARY
or
INTELLIGENCE SUMMARY.
(Erase heading not required.)

Army Form C. 2118.

Instructions regarding War Diaries and Intelligence Summaries are contained in F.S. Regs., Part II. and the Staff Manual respectively. Title pages will be prepared in manuscript.

Place	Date	Hour	Summary of Events and Information	Remarks and references to Appendices
LESTREM Sector	1/9/18		Quiet day on the line. Later company relief during night 1/2nd. B Company relieved D in advanced position. Battalion outpost posts gave a screen on LABIETTE FARM in the evening which has to be cut about in advance of enemy positions.	Appendix I
	2/9/18		C.O. visited the line in the morning with the Army Machine Gun Officer. A Company relieved D Company in PARADISE ROAD during night 2/3rd.	Appendix II
	3/9/18		During the morning, troops 59th Div attacked in conjunction with 19th & 61st to reached the line ESTAIRES — LA BASSÉE ROAD.	
	4/9/18		Battalion Headquarters moved from LABIETTE FARM to house at junction of LOCON ROAD & LOCK LANE. C Company withdrew from position in ROTENTUN LINE & concentration in billets in RUBECQ area. B Company moved forward with infantry & occupied headquarters at LE MARAIS E POST. A Company moved forward from PARADISE ROAD to LESTREM.	Appendix III

Army Form C. 2118.

WAR DIARY
or
INTELLIGENCE SUMMARY.
(Erase heading not required.)

Instructions regarding War Diaries and Intelligence Summaries are contained in F. S. Regs., Part II. and the Staff Manual respectively. Title pages will be prepared in manuscript.

Place	Date	Hour	Summary of Events and Information	Remarks and references to Appendices
LESTREM Section	5/9/18		C & D Companies moved from billets in ROGERS area to lines immediately W of LESTREM. In conjunction with infantry B Coy with gun moved forward. Line reached by our troops RUE TILLELOY. A Company took out line of Retention with guns at MUDDY LANE POST, LE DRUMEZ POST, CARTERS POST, RIEZ BAILLEUL & BOUT DEVILLE. Company H.Q. remained in LESTREM. 2nd Lieut R.W. Rye, R.J. Roberts, J. Melville & M. Parker & a draft of 62 NCOs & men reported to battalion.	Offensive IV
"	6/9/18		Quiet day. Line has become more or less stationary. B Company overpressed Headquarters near junction of LYDDITE LANE and GURNEY ROAD. Guns were disposed as follows. No 1 section 4 guns in about LAVENTIE. No 2 Sect 2 guns at DUD HOUSE & R. ESQUIN POST. No 3 Sect 2 guns in WANGERIE POST & 2 men junction of GUN COTTON LANE & FLINQUE ROAD No 4 Sect. 2 guns at LONELY POST & 2 at MILL POST.	
LAVENTIE Section	7/9/18		Hostile Artillery most active during the day. LAVENTIE & WANGERIE POST shelled. Harrassing fire was carried out on V.C. Ames. A. Coy moved to positions in new line of Retention about 400 yds E of ESTAIRES – LA BASSÉE ROAD. Company Head quarters near PONT. MARAIS.	
"	8/9/18		Enemy artillery active during afternoon & night. ESQUIN POST shelled between 3pm & 9pm. Harrassing fire carried out during night by B Coy on V.C. Ames DELVAS ROAD & BEE POST	

Army Form C. 2118.

WAR DIARY
or
INTELLIGENCE SUMMARY.
(Erase heading not required.)

Instructions regarding War Diaries and Intelligence Summaries are contained in F. S. Regs., Part II. and the Staff Manual respectively. Title pages will be prepared in manuscript.

Place	Date	Hour	Summary of Events and Information	Remarks and references to Appendices
LAVENTIE Sector	9/9/18		Quiet day. Heavy rain storms throughout the day. D Company took over half of A Coy gun in Main Battle line. D Company Headquarters at LE MARAIS E. Post. Lt-Col W J Rankin MC. leave to UK	Appendix V
"	10/9/18		Quiet Day. Heavy rain continued C Company relieves B Company in outpost position during tonight. Enemy artillery more active during the night especially on forward area E of ESTAIRES- LA BASSEE Road. H.V. gun shelled LESTREM area throughout night	Appendix VI
"	11/9/18		Heavy rain still continued. Hostile artillery was fairly active during the day + night. Harassing fire was carried out by C Company on VC corner + Two Yaw Farm	

Army Form C. 2118.

WAR DIARY
or
INTELLIGENCE SUMMARY.
(Erase heading not required.)

Instructions regarding War Diaries and Intelligence Summaries are contained in F. S. Regs., Part II. and the Staff Manual respectively. Title pages will be prepared in manuscript.

Place	Date	Hour	Summary of Events and Information	Remarks and references to Appendices
LAVENTIE Sector	12/9/18		Between 5am & 5.30am a field on VC Corner & roads in vicinity in enemy's wire and front line carried out by 61st Division on our left. Quiet day. Harassing fire was carried out by C Company on TWO TREE FARM, V.C. CORNER & Hostile M.G. near TRIVELET. Lt. W.G. Sturdee went to U.K.	
"	13/9/18		During the day B Company moved from PARADIS area to east near CLIFTON N. POST. Hostile Artillery fairly active throughout the day. LAVENTIE - CROIX BARBEE shelled during evening. C Company carried out harassing fire on TWO TREE FARM. RUE DELVAS & DISTILLERY.	
"	14/9/18		Quiet day. During the night back area & roads shelled intermittently. LAVENTIE shelled with 4.2" & 5.9". Harassing fire was carried out by C Company on V.C. Corner & TWO TREE FARM.	

WAR DIARY
or
INTELLIGENCE SUMMARY.

Army Form C. 2118.

Place	Date	Hour	Summary of Events and Information	Remarks and references to Appendices
LAVENTIE Sector	15/9/16		Enemy artillery quiet during day. LAVENTIE shelled intermittently throughout the night. C Company carried out harassing fire during the night on VC Corner & neighbourhood.	
"	16/9/16		Much better weather. Quiet day in the line. Throughout night hostile artillery became more active. Rennie's farm area shelled. Harassing fire was carried out by C Company on VC Corner, Two Tree Farm & LE FAUQUISSART Road in the neighbourhood of LA DISTILLERY. Capt. L.J.O. Simpson went to U.K.	
"	17/9/16		Quiet day. A Company took part in a Brigade scheme during the morning. Hostile artillery fairly active during the night. C Company carried out harassing fire on VC Corner, Two Tree Farm & neighbourhood of Distillery.	
"	18/9/16		Hostile artillery fairly quiet during day. Back area shelled during the night. Naval harassing fire carried out by C Company during the night. Targets included VC Corner & TRIVELET.	

WAR DIARY or INTELLIGENCE SUMMARY

Army Form C. 2118.

Place	Date	Hour	Summary of Events and Information	Remarks and references to Appendices
LAVENTIE Sector	19/9/18		Hostile shelling throughout the day. LAVENTIE shelled at intervals during the night. TWO TREE Farm & VC Corner engaged and harassing fire during the night.	
"	20/9/18		Quiet day. Scattered shelling throughout the day & night. Harassing fire was carried out by C Company on targets including TWO TREE FARM TRIVELET, in conjunction with a Brigade operation by 17 Bgde. Casualties 3 O.R. wounded.	
"	21/9/18		Hostile shelling was active at intervals during the afternoon neighbourhood of LE DRUMEZ POST was shelled until 5.9". LAVENTIE & ESTAIRES shelled during the evening. D Company relieved C Company in Outpost zone during the evening. B Company carried out harassing fire on VC CORNER & TWO TREE FARM.	Appendix V
"	22/9/18		With the exception of intermittent shelling by hostile artillery the day was quiet. B Company did not carry out harassing fire owing to forward section moving forward to new position.	

WAR DIARY
or
INTELLIGENCE SUMMARY.
(Erase heading not required.)

Army Form C. 2118.

Place	Date	Hour	Summary of Events and Information	Remarks and references to Appendices
LAVENTIE Sector	23/9/18		Intermittent shelling throughout the day. A few bombs were dropped by enemy aeroplanes during the night on back areas. B Company carried out the usual harassing fire on BEE POST, TROU POST, & TWO TREE FARM.	
"	24/9/18		Hostile Artillery was rather more active. Several battery positions & roads were shelled during the day. Harassing fire was carried out by B Company on SEEDS LODGE, TWO TREE FARM & roads in vicinity. Reinf. Lt. Col. Geo. Trace to U.K.	
"	25/9/18		Throughout the day enemy artillery was active. Y.C. Corner, BEE POST, TWO TREE FARM & roads in vicinity were fired on by B Company's night firing guns.	
"	26/9/18		C Company relieved A Company in left sector of Main Line of Relestance during the morning. Hostile artillery was very quiet during the day but became active during the night. B Company fired on gaps in enemy wire & new work.	Appendix VIII
"	29/9/18		Hostile Artillery quiet during the day. Harried activity during the night. Neighbourhood of HARROW POST shelled between 10pm & 1am by about 150 f.25 and 5.9m Gas ma in M.3.d. + M.19.b. and heavies by 5.9. B Coy fired harassing fire on new work and gaps in wire in N.7.9.a. + N.13.d.	

WAR DIARY
or
INTELLIGENCE SUMMARY.
(Erase heading not required.)

Army Form C. 2118.

Place	Date	Hour	Summary of Events and Information	Remarks and references to Appendices
27.10.18 cont	27.9.18 cont		Pres. Dallon leaves to U.K.	
LAVENTIE Sector	28.9.18		Our M.Guns engaged V.C. CORNER and EXETER AVENUE, also gaps in wire, firing 8000 rounds harassing fire. Hostile artillery fire on LAVENTIE E. POST, WANGUERIE, and Pt. d'ESQUIN during the night. Low flying enemy plane over our lines 5.30 pm. Lt. NORTH leave to U.K.	
	29.9.18		Our M.Guns fired 1500 rounds on V.C. CORNER and gaps in Wire. Hostile artillery active during the day — Gas shells on M/d from 6.30 pm. Slight Gas shelling during the night. Lt Col Falkiner returns from leave U.K. Lt. Levin goes to U.K. on Course	
	30.9.18		Our M Guns cooperate with Lewis Gunners at dawn. Rear B Coy and Scan. B Guns of C Coy relieve B Coy Lewis IX in forward trenches. Our Mg have engaged hostile working parties during the night. Hostile artillery below normal 8pm — 20.1.20 on M.234. Large Strap about 11pm on our Cavendish line. Capt Ganderiche Just returns from leave U.K.	

S E C R E T   Copy No. 18

NO. 25. BATTALION, MACHINE GUN CORPS.

BATTALION ORDER NO. 35.

Ref. Sheet. 36.A.N.E.) 1.20.000.   1st September.1918
     "   36A.S.E.)

1. "B" Company will relieve "D" Company in Outpost positions during night of 1st/2nd Sept: 1918.
    On relief "B" Company will come under orders of G.O.C. Advanced Guard Brigade.

2. On relief "D" Company will move back to the area vacated by "B" Company and will be attached to the Support Brigade.

3. All details of Relief to be arranged between O's C. "B" & "D" Companies.

4. Maps and Machine Gun Policy will be handed over by O.C. "D" Company.

5. O.C. "B" Company will get in touch with G.O.C. Advanced Guard Brigade on receipt of these orders.

6. Relief to be completed before Dawn on 2nd Sept:1918.

7. Relief Complete will be wired to Battn' H.Q, using Code Words "FATHER IS ALRIGHT".

8. "A" Company will be prepared to relieve "D" Company in Support Area on the night of 2nd/3rd Sept. Further Orders will be issued.

9. A C K N O W L E D G E. (Companies only.)

                                                    Major.
Issued at 1 pm by D.R.   No.25,Battn' Machine Gun Corps.
Distribution:-
   Copy. No.1.   C.O.   Copy.No.11. 176th Infty Bde.
    "   " 2.   2nd in Command.   "   12.   177th   "   "
    "   " 3.   O.C. A.Company.   "   13.   178th   "   "
    "   " 4.   O.C. B.   "   "   14.   59th Division."G"
    "   " 5.   O.C. C.   "   "   15.   61st M.G. Battn.
    "   " 6.   O.C. D.   "   "   16.   19th   "   "
    "   " 7.   Signalling Officer. "   17.   File.
    "   " 8.   Quartermaster.   "   18/19. War Diary.
    "   " 9.   Transport Officer.
    "   " 10.   R.S.M.

SECRET   Copy No. 18

Appendix II

NO. 25 BATTALION, MACHINE GUN CORPS.

BATTALION ORDER NO 36.

Ref. Sheet   36.A.N.E.) 1.20,000
     "   36.A.S.E.)

1. "A" Company will relieve "D" Company (H.Q.-Q.18.a.20.80.) in Support Area tonight.

2. "A" Company will move from billets at 5-0 pm. Route followed will be ST VENANT ST FLORIS CORNET MALO CALONNE.

3. Traffic Regulations No.G.27/11/11 will be complied with.

4. O.C. "A" Company will make himself acquainted with M.G. policy of Support Brigade and will report to G.O.C. Support Brigade at Q.4.c.

5. Bolt Boxes will not be handed over.

6. O.C. "A" Company will at once send on an Officer to arrange do and take over bivouacs and transport accomodation.

7. One officer from "A" Company and 1 O.R. per section will be le present billets to hand over to "D" Company on arrival.

8. Relief to be completed by 8-30 pm.

9. Relief complete will be notified to this office, using the code "MOTHER."

10. Acknowledge.

Issued at 4-50 pm by D.R.   J. H. Williams, Ma
Distribution :-   No 25 Battalion, Machine Gun
 Copy No. 1.   C.O.
  "   "   2.   ~~2nd. in Command~~ Adjt.   Copy No 11   176th Infty. Bdo.
  "   "   3.   O.C. A Company   "   " 12   177th   "   "
  "   "   4.   O.C. B   "   "   " 13   178th   "   "
  "   "   5.   O.C. C   "   "   " 14   59th Division "G"
  "   "   6.   O.C. D   "   "   " 15   61st. M.G. Battn.
  "   "   7.   Signalling Officer   "   " 16   19th M.G. Battn.
  "   "   8.   Quartermaster   "   " 17   File
  "   "   9.   Transport Officer   " 18/19   War Diary.
  "   " 10.   R.S.M.

War Diary *Appendix III*

SECRET   Copy No. 19

No. 25 BATTALION, MACHINE GUN CORPS.

BATTALION ORDER NO 37.

Reference Sheet   36 A.N.E.) 1;20,000
            "   36 A.S.E.)

1. Battalion Headquarters will move forward tomorrow to R.15.b.95.40.

2. This office will close at LABIETTE FARM at 12-0 noon and open at the same time at R.15.b.95.40.

3. Personnel of Headquarter Company as detailed to R.S.M. will parade at 8-40 am.ready to move off.
The R.S.M. will be in charge of this party.

4. Details of transport will be as follows :-

    Mess Cart   at H.Q. Mess at 8-30 am.
    G.S.Waggon   "   "   "   at 8-30 am.
    R.E. Limbered Waggon at H.Q. at 8-30 am.
    Orderly Room Limber at H.Q. at 8-15 am.

5. The Transport Officer will reconnoitre the area Q.12,18,24. for accomodation for transport and will move up the remaining transport under his own arrangements.

6. "C" Company will withdraw from their present positions IN the RETENTION LINE,during morning 4th.September,and will concentrate in billets in the neighbourhood of ROBECQ. Exact position of H.Q. will be notified to Battalion Headquarters.

7. "D" Company will move into billets vacated by Battalion Headquarters during the afternoon of September 4th.

Issued at 11-5 PM by D.R.   Major.
                                                       No.25 Battalion,Machine Gun Corps.

Distribution :-

Copy No			Copy No	
" " 1	C.O.		11	176th Infantry Brigade.
" " 2	Adjt.		12	177th " "
" " 3	O.C. A Company		13	178th " "
" " 4	O.C. B "		14	59th Division "G"
" " 5	O.C. C "			61st M.G.Battn. (15)
" " 6	O.C. D "		16	19th M.G.Battn
" " 7	Signalling Officer		17	File
" " 8	Quartermaster		18/19	War Diary.
" " 9	Transport Officer			
" " 10	R.S.M.			

SECRET
War Diary Appendix VI
Copy No. 18

NO. 25 BATTALION. MACHINE GUN CORPS.

BATTALION ORDER NO.39

Reference Sheets :
    36.A.S.E. & 36.S.W. 1:20,000

9th September.

1. "C" Company, 25th Battn. M.G. Corps will relieve "B" Company 25th Battalion. M.G. Corps, in the OUTPOST ZONE on September 10th, 1918. Relief to be complete by 7-0 pm.

2. O.C. "C" Company will make himself thoroughly acquainted with all details of Machine Gun Policy before relief.

3. On completion of relief O.C. "C" Company will come under the orders of G.O.C. Advanced Guard Brigade, to whom he should report.

4. All details of relief will be arranged between OsC. Companies concerned.

5. On completion of relief "B" Company will take over bivouacs at present occupied by "C" Company.

6. Completion of relief to be notified to Battalion Headquarters as under :-

    No unusual shelling .... NO
    Heavy shelling............... YES
    Relief complete.............. PAPA.

7. Acknowledge.

------------------------------- Major
No. 25 Battalion. Machine Gun Corps

Issued at 12.30pm by D.R.
Distribution.

Copy No 1 C.O.	Copy No 7. Signalling Officer
2. Adjt.	8. Transport Officer
3. O.C. "A" Company	9. Quartermaster
4. O.C. "B" "	10. R.S.M.
5. O.C. "C" "	11. 59th. Division "G"
6. O.C. "D" "	12. 176th Infantry Bde.
	13. 177th Infantry Bde.
	14. 178th Infantry Bde.
	15. 61st. M.G. Battalion.
	16. 19th M.G. Battalion.
	17. File.
	18 and 19 War Diary.

G 14/3
9.9.18

SECRET   Copy No. 18

NO. 25 BATTALION. MACHINE GUN CORPS.

BATTALION ORDER NO 40.

Ref.Sheets. 36.A.S.E. & 36.S.W. 1:20,000   9th September 18.

1.   The main BATTLE LINE is being held by two Brigades.

2.   The main BATTLE LINE now runs as follows :-
ROUGE-CROIX (exclusive)-PONT-du-HEM- LE DRUMEZ POST to Divisional Boundary about G.35.a.6.3.

3.   The Dividing line between Brigades in the BATTLE LINE is the E. and W. grid line between squares M.9. and M.15.

4.   Under Divisional Instructions 1 Machine Gun Company is to be attached to each Brigade in the BATTLE LINE.

5.   Brigade Headquarters will be :-
Right Sub-sector........R.11.d.4.2.
Left Sub-sector........R.10.a.4.0.

6.   In accordance with above "D" Company, 25th Battalion.M.G.Corps will relieve the following guns of "A" Company:-

1. M.9.c.10.20   5.) M.15.d.05.35.
2. M.9.c.20.80   6.)
3. M.9.c.47.44.   7. M.21.a.22.25.
4. M.9.d.25.25   8. M.21.c.22.20.

7.   O's C. Companies will then dispose their remaining guns in accordance with the principles of defence in depth.

8.   O's.C. Companies will report to their respective Brigades to ensure liaison between the machine guns and infantry in their respective sub-sectors.

9.   Relief to be complete by 8-0 pm. September 10th.18.

10.   Completion of relief to be reported to Battalion Headquarters as under :-
Heavy shelling..............BANG
No unusual shelling.........THE
Relief Complete.............DRUM

11.   A C K N O W L E D G E. (Companies only)

                                    A Wworth Lt
                                    for Major.
Issued at 1.06pm by D.R.   No 25 Battalion.Machine Gun Corps.
Distribution :-

Copy No 1 C.O.   10. R.S.M.
       2   Adjutant   11. 58th Division "G"
       3   O.C. "A" Company   12. 176th Infantry Brigade
       4. O.C. "B"   "   13. 177th Infantry Brigade
       5. O.C. "C"   "   14. 178th Infantry Brigade
       6. O.C. "D"   "   15. 61st. M.G.Battalion.
       7. Signalling Officer   16. 19th M.G.Battalion.
       8. Transport Officer   17. FILE
       9. Quartermaster   18 & 19 WAR DIARY.

SECRET   Copy No. 18

No 25 BATTALION. MACHINE GUN CORPS.

BATTALION ORDER NO 41

Reference Sheets :-
36.A.S.E. & 36.S.W. 1:20,000.   20th.September.18.

1. "B" Company, 25th. Battalion.M.G.C. will relieve "C" Coy, 25th. Battalion.M.G.C. in the OUTPOST ZONE, on September 21st,1918. Relief to be complete by 7-0 pm.

2. O.C. "B" Company will make himself thoroughly acquainted with all details of M.G. Policy before relief.

3. On completion of relief O.C. "B" Company will come under orders of G.O.C. Advanced Guard Brigade, to whom he should report.

4. All details of relief will be arranged between O.s C. Companies concerned.

5. On completion of relief "C" Company will take over Huts, etc, at present occupied by "B" Company.

6. All maps, aeroplane photographs, etc., will be handed over and receipt obtained by O.C. "C" Company.

7. Completion of relief will be notified to Battalion Headquarters as under :-

    No unusual shelling............PRESS
    Heavy shelling.................THE
    Relief complete................BUTTON.

8. ACKNOWLEDGE (Companies only).

                                                          Major.
                                    Commanding No.25 Battalion.M.G.Corps.

Issued at 7.15 pm. by D.R.

DISTRIBUTION.

Copy No.1	C.O.	10.	R.S.M.
2.	Adjt.	11.	59th. Division."G"
3.	O.C. "A" Company.	12.	176th. Inf. Brigade.
4.	O.C. "B" Company	13.	177th. Inf. Brigade
5.	O.C. "C" Company	14.	178th. Infantry Brigade.
6.	O.C. "D" Company.	15.	61st. M.Gun Battn.
7.	Signalling Officer	16.	19th. M.Gun Battn.
8.	Transport Officer	17.	FILE
9.	Quartermaster.	18 &19	War Diary.

SECRET.   Copy No. 18

No 25 BATTALION MACHINE GUN CORPS.

BATTALION ORDER No 42.

Reference Sheets:-
36A N.E. & 36. S.W. 1:20,000   25th September 1918.

1. "A" Company will be relieved by "C" Company in the Main Line of Resistance on September 26th. Relief to be complete by 2 p.m.

2. O.C. "C" Company will make himself fully acquainted with all details of M.G. policy in the line.

3. Maps, Range Cards and all Trench Stores will be handed over and copies of receipts sent to Battalion H.Q. by 6 p.m. September 27th.

4. On relief "A" Company will take over the camp vacated by "C" Company.

5. All other details of relief will be arranged between O's C. Companies concerned.

6. Relief complete will be notified to Battalion Headquarters using the code :-

        No unusual shelling:..... BUY
        Heavy shelling:........... OUR
        Relief Complete:......... BUTTER

9. ACKNOWLEDGE (Companies only).

                                                                                  Major.
                Commdg. No 25 Battalion. Machine Gun Corps.

Issued at 5.15/m by D.R.

DISTRIBUTION.

Copy No. 1.	C.O.	10.	R.S.M.
2.	Adjutant.	11.	50th. Division "G".
3.	O.C. "A" Company	12.	176th. Infantry Bde.
4.	O.C. "B" Company	13.	177th. Infantry Bde.
5.	O.C. "C" Company	14.	178th. Infantry Bde.
6.	O.C. "D" Company	15.	61st. M.G. Battalion.
7.	Signalling Officer.	16.	10th. M.G. Battalion.
8.	Transport Officer	17.	File.
9.	Quartermaster.	18 & 19	War Diary.

--o-o-o-o-o-o-o-o-o-o-o-o-

www.ingramcontent.com/pod-product-compliance
Lightning Source LLC
Chambersburg PA
CBHW081456160426
43193CB00013B/2498